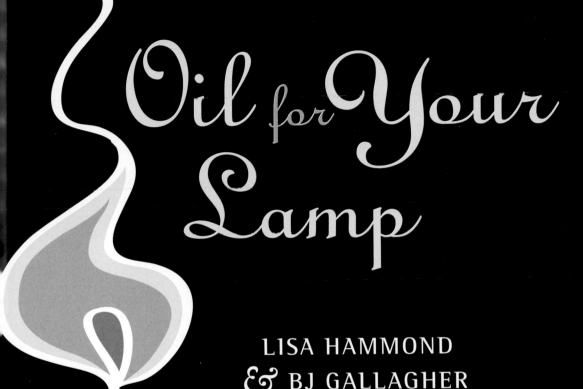

Oil for Your Lamp

LISA HAMMOND
& BJ GALLAGHER

simple truths®

Published by SimpleTruths, LLC
1952 McDowell Road, Suite 300
Naperville, Illinois 60563

Design and production: Koechel Peterson & Associates, Inc., Minneapolis, MN

Edited by: ST Editing Team

Simple Truths is a registered trademark.

Printed and bound in United States of America

800-900-3427
www.simpletruths.com

05 WOZ 13

TABLE of CONTENTS

"*To keep a lamp burning, we have to keep putting oil in it.*" ~MOTHER TERESA, humanitarian

I Believe Women Are A Lot Like Lamps.

Over the last 40 years, research studies have shown that women's overall level of happiness has dropped. This decline in happiness has no connection to whether or not we have kids, how healthy we are, what career we choose, what our income is, how old we are or whether we are single or divorced. The bottom line is: Women are losing ground on the happiness scale. I think it's because we are out of oil.

When we see women who shine, they all have one thing in common—they know that self-care is the first step to happiness. These women understand the importance of eating right, getting enough sleep, taking time to play and investing in supportive relationships.

Recently, I tuned in to a TV interview with Ellen DeGeneres. Her radiance beamed from the screen. I thought to myself, *Now there is a woman who has learned how to fill up her lamp.* She not only tells all of us to live life to the fullest, to love, dance and laugh every day—she clearly does so herself. Her lamp is full and glowing brightly!

Throughout the pages of this book, BJ and I will share stories from women who have let their lamps run on fumes ... and contrast them with women who have learned how to refuel, keeping their lamps burning brightly.

Lisa Hammond, The Barefoot CEO, Femail Creations

HOW AND WHY WE LET THE OIL IN OUR LAMPS RUN LOW

Virtually every woman we know has the same problem—she knows what's good for her, but she often doesn't do it. She knows she should eat less and exercise more, but still she doesn't make healthy choices. She knows she needs to spend her time and money more effectively, but good time and money management elude her. She finds herself always putting others first, while neglecting her own needs and wants. She doesn't get enough rest or sleep; her endless to-do list hangs overhead like the sword of Damocles; and sometimes she doesn't even take time to pee! As our friend Brenda Knight laments frequently, "Why am I always riding in the back of my own bus?"

We don't do the things we know are good for us because we are so busy taking care of others that we neglect ourselves. The problem isn't lack of information—we have plenty of information about the importance of sleep, healthy foods and exercise. The problem is how we prioritize our lives.

Psychologists tell us that some people are inner-directed and some are other-directed. That is, some people focus on their own internal guidance system for making choices about how to spend their time and energy. Their own self-interest ranks very high on their list of priorities. "What's best for me?" is a key guiding principle in determining where they focus their attention and how they make day-to-day decisions.

And some people are other-directed, which means that their primary focus is external, not internal. They are primarily concerned with relationships, especially people they care about. "How can I help others?" is a key question in how they spend their time and energy. Building and nurturing relationships with loved ones, family, friends, neighbors and coworkers is the guiding principle in their lives.

Research indicates that, in general, men tend to be more inner-directed, while women tend to be more other-directed. There are exceptions, of course, but as a group, men are focused on

themselves while women are focused on other people. Men like to build things while women like to build relationships.

This difference in psychological orientation goes a long way toward helping us understand why we women often do such a poor job of taking care of ourselves. We run around filling others' lamps with oil, but forget to fill our own lamps first. Then we wonder why we're often exhausted, frazzled, stressed-out, anxious and/or depressed!

Awareness is the first step toward solving a problem. So the first section of this book is devoted to helping us acknowledge the problem and understand the reasons for it. Chapter 1 looks at how girls are socialized, growing up to be women who put others first. Chapter 2 examines the values women have adopted in the past 50 years, beginning with the feminist movement—leading us to believe that we can have it all—all at once. And Chapter 3 explores the corresponding myth that we can DO it all.

But don't be discouraged. Help is on the way—in Section II, we'll get into solutions for the problem. We'll learn the value of doing nothing, how to play again, how to become more inner-directed, and most importantly, how to ask for help.

CHAPTER 1

SOCIALIZED TO PUT EVERYONE ELSE FIRST

"Life is a process of becoming, a combination of states we have to go through. Where people fail is that they wish to elect a state and remain in it. This is a kind of death."

~ANAÏS NIN, French-born diarist

What I Want Matters, Too.

by MICHELLE SEDAS

I chose finance as my major in college. It was a good, respectable major and I wanted my parents to be proud of me. After I graduated from college, I married and chose a solid, steady job in the financial services industry. This time, I wanted both my parents and my husband to be proud of me. The problem with this job was that dealing with customer service issues all day long didn't suit my personality. At the time, my husband was traveling a lot and most evenings, dreading the calls filled with irritated customers that inevitably the next day would bring, I'd find myself in tears.

After a year of working in this job, I quit and traveled with my husband wherever his company sent him. I thought that just being close to my husband would solve everything and would bring back my passion for life. Over time, as we traveled, I began to dread interacting with others. I was overly self-conscious. I would go out of my way so that I wouldn't have to talk to strangers. And at the time, everyone was a stranger to me. It got to the point where I had completely lost my passion. I found myself staying alone in the apartment all day long and I had become so reclusive that it would take hours to build up the courage to venture out alone. Eventually, I was hospitalized for depression.

Upon recovering from this depressive episode, I knew that I needed to reassess my priorities and the way that I was living. My husband and I settled back into my hometown in the Dallas/Fort Worth area. I began making connections with friends again. I started interviewing for jobs. The time came when I had to choose between a full-time bank job and a part-time job in customer service at a publishing company, which didn't require a college degree, but would have me surrounded with one of my passions: books. My first reaction was to take the bank job. After all, I wanted my parents to feel that their college dollars had been well spent. But then I looked deeper.

What did I want to do? Which job would I be the most passionate about? Where would I find the most joy? The answer was obvious: *the publishing company.*

It's a choice that I've never regretted once. Within this company, I moved from customer service, to editing, to eventually writing books, and becoming the host of the Inspired Living Café, where I write a weekly newsletter. I couldn't imagine a job more suited to my personality. I couldn't imagine being anywhere else. And my passion for life came back when I realized that what I wanted mattered, too.

What
did I want
to do?

Women As Caregivers

In 2003, 50.3 percent of adult women were married and living with a spouse. Over 10 percent of women were the head of a household, meaning that they had children or other relatives living in their household, but no spouse. Another 16.6 percent of adult women lived in the home of a parent or other relative. Almost 15 percent of adult women lived alone, and nearly seven percent were living with non-relatives.

Women often function as caregivers for the people with whom they live, or for other relatives or friends. One out of every four people is a caregiver for a family member or friend, and, in the absence of an able spouse, a daughter or daughter-in-law is most likely to assume the role of caregiver.* Approximately 75 percent of caregivers for older family members and friends are female.** Of the 2.4 million grandparents who live with and are responsible for grandchildren, 63 percent are women.

* U.S. Department of Health and Human Services, Administration on Aging. Snapshot: National Family Caregiver Support Program. August 2003.
** Family Caregiver Alliance. Selected caregiver statistics. http://www.caregiver.org

WAKING UP

by BJ GALLAGHER

When I was a young wife, I used to iron my husband's shirts every week. He was a snappy dresser and meticulous about his clothes. One weekend he happened to be watching me as I ironed.

"Why do you do it that way?" he asked.

"What?" I replied. "This is just the way it's done."

"Really?" he asked.

"Well, sure," I responded. "You start with the collar and iron that. Then you do the part across the shoulders. Then you iron one sleeve, and the other. Finally, you start on the front side with the buttons and work your way around to the back of the shirt and end on the front side with the button holes. That's the way it's done."

Seemingly amused, he asked, "Who says?"

"Well, that's the way my mother did it," I answered. And it suddenly occurred to me that I ironed shirts the way my mother did without ever even thinking about it! It's as if I absorbed things by osmosis without even being conscious of all I was taking in. I wondered how many other things I just did automatically because that's the way it was done in my family.

Scary thought, to discover that you're living by rote—on automatic pilot—like a programmed robot, unthinking, unconscious.

That day was a long time ago and since then I've become a lot more conscious. It's as if I fell asleep when I was born and it's taken me all these years to slowly awaken.

I'm grateful for events and things that cause me to question the values and assumptions I accepted without question for so many years; incidents, comments, and people who jolt me into new states of awareness. And awareness is the first step to change. Today, I choose to live consciously and examine my habits in order to shed those that no longer serve me.

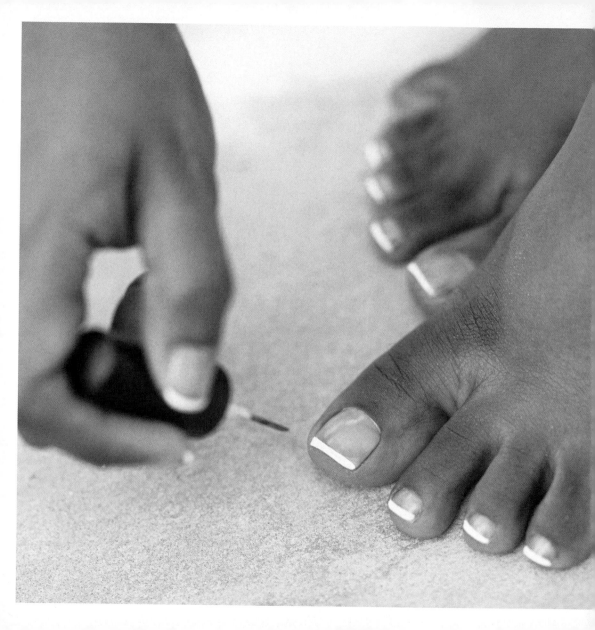

I WAS TAUGHT

by BJ GALLAGHER

When I was a girl
I asked my mother
why she polished her nails.
    "Your father likes it,"
      she said.

She cooked his favorite dinner
when he came home from a trip
and served him
    the biggest and best portions
      at every meal.

She taught me
    to treat a man like a king.

[CONTINUED...]

When I went to school
the teachers said,
        "It's good to share
        and play well with others."

"No one will like you
        if you're not nice."

They taught me to be
        "a good team player."

When I was a teen
I read the girls' magazines.
The stories explained that
        boys like girls
        who are cheerful and fun—
                not girls who are sad or mad.

They taught me to
        put on a happy face.

[CONTINUED...]

Share

When I went to church
the ministers preached,
        "It's better to give
        than receive."

"Self-sacrifice is a virtue
        and martyrdom is noble."

They seemed to say that
        self-love is self*ish*.

I was taught by others
what it means to be a woman
        and I learned my lessons well.

So why am I tired,
        angry,
                and resentful?

Why do I feel that I never measure up,
        no matter how much I do?

Is it any wonder I'm confused?

I was taught so many things
        by so many people...

Could they all be wrong?

CHAPTER 2

MULTI-TASKING
MAVENS

" You need not feel guilty about not being able to keep your life perfectly balanced. Juggling everything is too difficult. All you really need to do is catch it before it hits the floor!"

~CAROL BARTZ, CEO, Yahoo!

Pumpkin

by LISA HAMMOND

I always wanted to be the best mom in the world—but I've rarely been able to live up to that standard. I stayed at home when my kids were little and didn't start my business until they were both in school. When my daughter Harlie was in fifth grade and my son Bridger in kindergarten, I gave birth to my new business. I had so much going on—kids, husband, home, and now, a start-up. What I *didn't* have was sleep!

I recall it was late October and I was scrambling to get ready for my first serious holiday season at work. Bridger's teacher had scheduled a Halloween party for his class. Since I am not

Martha Stewart, rather than sew Bridger's Halloween costume, I ordered it from a catalog. On the day of the party I got Bridger all dressed up in his green tights, green shoes, bright orange round pumpkin and matching stem hat. He looked adorable. We raced out the door and I dropped him off at school on my way to the office.

I had only been at work for about five minutes when I received a phone call—it was the school. Bridger was on the phone in tears. "Mom, you had the wrong day!" he sobbed. "The Halloween party is *tomorrow!*" He was the only child at school in a costume. He had been hiding in the bathroom when his teacher found him. Now I was in tears, too.

I made the "drive of shame" home to get Bridger's school uniform and then back to the school so he could change. I'll never forget this angry little boy—dressed like a pumpkin—waiting for me when I got back to the school. The look on his face still haunts me and I cringe when I think about it—a "bad mother" day, for sure! 🍂

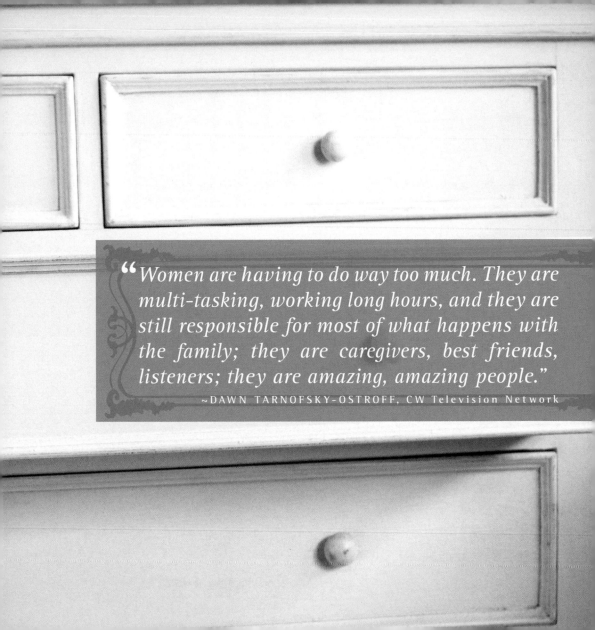

> "*Women are having to do way too much. They are multi-tasking, working long hours, and they are still responsible for most of what happens with the family; they are caregivers, best friends, listeners; they are amazing, amazing people.*"
>
> ~DAWN TARNOFSKY-OSTROFF, CW Television Network

Women Who Work

[1] In 2006, a record 67 million women were employed in the U.S.— 75 percent of employed women worked in full-time jobs, while 25 percent worked on a part-time basis.

[2] The largest percentage of employed women (38 percent) worked in management, professional, and related occupations; 34 percent worked in sales and office occupations; 20 percent in service occupations; 6 percent in production, transportation, and material moving occupations; and 1 percent in natural resources, construction, and maintenance occupations.

[3] The largest percentage of employed Asian and white women (46 percent and 39 percent, respectively) worked in management, professional, and related occupations. For African-American and Hispanic women, it was sales and office occupations—32 percent and 33 percent, respectively.

[4] The median weekly earnings of women who were full-time wage and salary workers was $600, or 81 percent of men's $743. When comparing the median weekly earnings of persons aged 16 to 24, young women earned 94 percent of what young men earned ($395 and $418, respectively).

5 Women accounted for 51 percent of all workers in the high-paying management, professional, and related occupations. They outnumbered men in such occupations as financial managers; human resource managers; education administrators; medical and health services managers; accountants and auditors; budget analysts; property, real estate, and social and community association managers; preschool, kindergarten, elementary, middle, and secondary school teachers; physical therapists; and registered nurses.

6 The higher a person's educational attainment, the more likely they will be a labor force participant (working or looking for work) and the less likely they will be unemployed.

SOURCE: U.S. Department of Labor, Bureau of Labor Statistics, Employment and Earnings, 2006 Annual Averages and the Monthly Labor Review, November 2005.

A MOVE WORTH MAKING

by LISA HAMMOND

When you read Oprah's magazine, she always has a section in the back about what she knows for sure. Whenever I see that, I am reminded of the times I haven't listened to my intuition and have lived to regret it. Every time I have taken advice from an "expert" because surely they must know more than I do, and it has gone against what my gut is telling me, I have wished I hadn't.

Women's intuition isn't a cliché. It is our best asset! And often when we are following our intuition people think we are foolish. They question our judgment. They doubt our decisions. And frankly they wonder if we have lost our minds.

When my friend Pam gave up a lucrative job most people would kill for, a lot of people thought she was crazy. But Pam was determined to find a way to travel less, stop multi-tasking and spend more time with her daughter. In order to do this, her new job would require a move from sunny Las Vegas, to chilly South Dakota. Yes, plenty of people questioned Pam's decision.

However, Pam didn't give up; she packed up the family and headed for South Dakota. She said, "My husband wasn't thrilled, my daughter was mad at me for making her leave her friends, and I didn't know if I would have enough courage to do it, but I dug deep and found the strength and off we went." In the end, it turned out to be the best two years of their lives. "It was a pivotal time for me, it was really the first time I ever learned how to say 'no,' to stand up for what I really believed was right for our family."

As Pam reflected back on that time when she had less on her plate, she said she was so happy she had been true to herself and her commitment to a simpler life and wondered why women have to get halfway through their lives in order to learn that.

"Life's challenges
are not supposed to paralyze you—
they're supposed to help you
discover who you are."

~BERNICE JOHNSON REAGON, songtalker

MULTI-TASKING

by BJ GALLAGHER

"Multi-tasking" doesn't do justice
to what women really do...
   miracle-working is more like it!

We keep the home fires burning
      while putting out fires at work.
We make to-do lists,
      grocery lists,
            and lists of assets and liabilities.
We wear our power suits,
      go power walking,
            eat power bars,
                  and power through our weekend chores.

We hold together our families,
      put together a cute outfit,
            pull together at work,
                  and glue together broken toys.

We juggle our time,
    projects,
        and
        commitments,
balance work and family
    as well as checkbooks.

And we do it all
    while looking our best.

My mother told me that
    "Women's work is never done."

Now I know why!

"The Golden Rule works for men as written, but for women it should go the other way around. We need to do unto ourselves as we do unto others."

~GLORIA STEINEM, feminist pioneer

CHAPTER 3

RUNNING ON EMPTY

> *I try to fill the emptiness deep inside me with Cheetos, but I am still depressed. Only now my fingers are stained orange. I am blue. And I am orange."*
>
> ~KAREN SALMANSOHN, author

Snap Out of It

by LISA HAMMOND

Over the years, as my dream of empowering and inspiring women and girls expanded and grew, so too did the time and energy required to fulfill that dream. As many entrepreneurs can relate, the "start up years" last far longer than can be imagined. I have joked that owning your own business means you can set your own hours—yep, you get to pick any 18 hours a day you want to work!

Rarely did I ever take a real day off. Even when I took a "vacation" the laptop, cell phone and work came with me. As the owner of the company, I was never off duty. After almost a decade like this, true exhaustion set in and health challenges were mounting. My body started refusing to comply with this inhumane schedule.

I wish I could report to you that as soon as my body spoke up, I listened. I want to tell you I wised up and started to take better care of myself. But that would be a lie. I am ashamed to admit while I was telling other women to nurture themselves, I was spreading myself far too thin.

The passion to help other women was stronger than the call to help myself and I unwisely started another business. Yet, even with the best infrastructure in place and devoting endless hours to the new business, it became a financial and emotional bottomless pit. It had finally depleted every ounce of energy I had left. It was a wake up call for me.

We all have to start with ourselves. It was time to walk my talk. I had to get serious about putting oil into my very depleted lamp. I began a journey of making very difficult decisions. I started removing things from my life that were not filling up my cup and adding things that brought joy back into

I was
never
off duty.

my life. Some changes were sweeping, other changes were small. I started cooking again and I started writing more, something I rarely had time for with my old work schedule. I tended to my garden, weeding out the draining things, and planting more of the things that replenished my spirit.

It wasn't easy for me to admit how far off track I had gotten. After all, it was my mission in life to inspire and empower other women, and here I was failing at that for myself. However, the gift of burnout, and a soul crying out for OIL, finally snapped even me out of it.

RUNNING *on* EMPTY

by BJ GALLAGHER

The warning light on my dashboard goes on.
"I can make it just a few more miles,"
       I think to myself,
            ignoring the warning light.

The balance in my checking account is ebbing low.
"I can squeak by until my next paycheck,"
       I tell myself,
            rationalizing my worry away.

My body is dragging, my energy flagging.
"I'll go to bed soon,
after I finish a few more things,"
    I tell myself,
        brushing off my fatigue.

Oh Self, how do I neglect thee?
    Let me count the ways ...

I put everyone else first—
    and myself last.

I take care of my loved ones—
    and forget to care for myself.

I over-commit to others—
    and bail out on commitments to myself.

I encourage and support my friends—
    but criticize and find fault with myself.

I love my neighbor—
    But neglect to love myself.

As I gaze in the mirror
    at my weary brow
        and tired eyes,
I realize that I've met the enemy—
    and she is me.

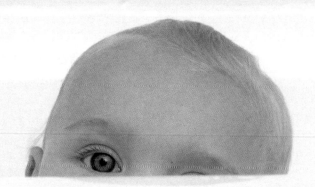

"Most people are so busy knocking themselves out trying to do everything they think they should do, they never get around to do what they want to do." ~KATHLEEN WINSOR, novelist

Perfectionism

by BJ GALLAGHER

Striving for excellence is not the same as striving for perfection. I don't need to become a driven, Type-A, maniacal perfectionist in order to feel good about myself. I simply strive for the highest standard that each situation calls for, to the best of my ability.

Few things in life need to be done perfectly—brain surgery is probably one of them—maybe human space shuttle missions, too—or work with hazardous radiation. But most everything else does not have the same exacting level of perfection. I am committed to doing the best job I can with the information and resources I have available, within the time allotted.

Being a great parent means knowing when to insist that your kids toe the line and when to let things slide. Being an achiever at work requires you to work with others, make the most of the time and energy you have, within certain budget constraints. Being committed to taking care of your body and health means educating yourself about nutrition, eating sensibly, making exercise a regular part of your life, and getting enough rest, as well as adequate medical care.

Being a terrific human being does not mean that you have to keep the perfect house, raise the perfect kids, have the perfect body, work at the perfect company in the perfect job. It simply means having the highest standards possible, appropriate to each situation.

Sometimes, if something is worth doing, it may be worth doing only modestly well ... if other more important things require a higher level of performance. Each of us must decide for ourselves which thing we need to do perfectly and which things we can simply do well.

As the old saying goes: "When all else fails, lower your standards." There's a lot of wisdom in that statement.

WOMEN WHO LIGHT UP the WORLD

by BJ GALLAGHER

We are women
who light up the world—
    with our beauty,
        our creativity,
            our intelligence,
                and charm.

Our eyes sparkle
    as we talk and laugh among ourselves.
Our smiles radiate warmth and comfort
    to those who love us.
Our faces beam happily
    when we're engaged in fulfilling work.

We shine,
    we illuminate,
        we enlighten,
            we dazzle.

We glow softly when contented—
    and burn brightly when passionate.
We are always lighting up the world,
    one way or another.

But who's the keeper of the flame?

Who will fill our lamps
        in order for us
                to light up the world?

We must do it for ourselves,
        dear sisters—
                and for each other.
We must fill our own lamps first,
        not last.

We must commit to our own well-being and self-care,
        lest our oil run low
                and our flames flicker out.

For a woman whose flame has extinguished
        can no longer fulfill her mission in life—
                lighting up the world.

So take some time,
        sweet sisters,
to rest,
        recoup,
                relax,
                        and regroup.

Take time
        to fill your lamp.

The world needs your flame—
        but first,
                you need your oil.

HOW TO
FILL OUR
OWN
LAMPS

Do you recognize yourself in the stories and poems in the first half of the book? Have you, too, found yourself multi-tasking until you thought you'd lose your mind from keeping too many plates spinning in the air? Have you ever forgotten your kid, or the family dog, or your spouse, because you were so distracted from a too-full schedule? Do you sometimes feel that you've been running on empty for so long that you're burned out?

If so, don't despair. Help is at hand. We've put our heads together and come up with some of the best tips we've both learned about how to fill our own lamps first—and keep them filled! Pick and choose some of the strategies and ideas that you'd like to adopt in your own life, then give them a try.

Our tips and tools fall into five categories:

[1] Put yourself at the top of your list.

[2] Learn to play again.

[3] Ask for help.

[4] Master the art of doing nothing.

[5] Recharge and Rejoice!

Read them and reap … great results! 🍃

CHAPTER 1

PUT YOURSELF AT THE TOP OF YOUR LIST

66 *Half of the troubles of this life can be traced to saying 'yes' too quickly and not saying 'no' soon enough."*

~JOSH BILLINGS, humorist and author

Today is Someday

by LISA HAMMOND

A few years ago I went through an experience that turned out to be life-changing. I woke up one morning feeling really dizzy and unable to focus. I grabbed my laptop and got back into bed figuring I would just start my day from there. I tried to answer a few e-mails but discovered my eyes just wouldn't cooperate. So I turned off my laptop and headed for the shower. I stopped to tweeze my eyebrows and that is when I actually saw my eyes—my mismatched eyes! One pupil was fully dilated and the other pupil was just a pinpoint.

Although it was very strange and I was really dizzy, I still went ahead and got in the shower. I had an important meeting at the office and I was still trying to get there on time.

The phone rang and it was my sister Diane wondering if I had read her e-mail yet. I told her I couldn't see my computer screen very well because my eyes were "wigging out." Alarmed, and wiser than me, she told me to get to the doctor immediately. So I called my husband to come home and drive me to the doctor.

My doctor examined me and then told me he feared this could be serious. After he left the room I could hear him out in the hall calling a specialist and telling them he was sending over an emergency patient.

When I got to the ophthalmologist, he examined me right away and tried all kinds of gadgets and eye drops. Yet nothing seemed to change anything and I was feeling worse and worse. He told me I needed to go to yet another doctor and called a neurologist asking her to see me immediately. By now, I was beginning to think that the "important meeting" I had at the office wasn't so important after all.

By the time we got to the neurologist, I wasn't as worried about what was going on as I was about getting my eyes back to normal so I would stop throwing up. After she examined me, she sent me off for an emergency MRI of my brain. She found a facility across town willing to stay open late to see me.

We got stuck in rush hour traffic, so we were even later than expected, yet when we arrived the staff was patiently waiting, and had even filled out part of my paper work for me. The woman who did the MRI could tell I wasn't coping too well with the claustrophobic face mask and the confined space and she kept reassuring me it would be over soon. Thirty minutes and two IVs later, it was.

We went back to the waiting room for what turned out to be the longest 20 minutes of my life. It was only then that I finally realized what I may be facing—a possible brain tumor, a stroke, or worse. I was being treated so kindly by the staff—the very staff I was keeping after hours. It was then I was sure I must be a dead woman walking.

The doctor finally called us back to review the films. He took a deep breath and said, "Well, your brain is normal." I asked him if I could get that in writing since there were plenty of people, including myself, who would question whether or not I was normal. My eyes may have made my face look like a Picasso painting, but I hadn't lost my sense of humor.

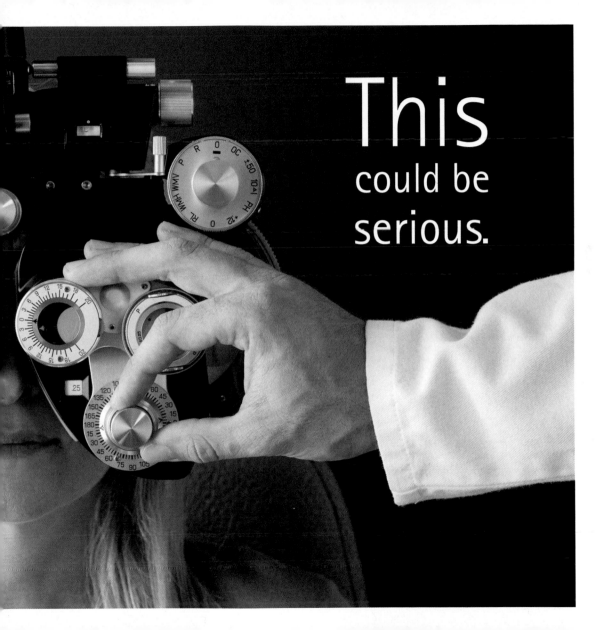

This
could be
serious.

After several more tests and lots of blood work, my neurologist determined that my symptoms stemmed from a very rare virus. It took about a week for my pupils to get completely back to the right size and for me to start feeling better. I soon went back to my normal hectic schedule.

About a month later, I went out of town on a business trip to the East Coast. The time change always throws my schedule off so I found myself up late trying to find some mindless TV to put me to sleep. As I flipped around the channels, suddenly, there appeared on the screen a woman talking about being diagnosed with a brain tumor—the same kind of brain tumor that I might have had. The program followed her from diagnosis through treatment. I watched for the next two hours as tears streamed down my face. Suddenly, the potential seriousness of my own problem hit me.

Why do we think these things only happen to *other people?* It is so easy to take our lives for granted. I am sure it was no accident that I was channel surfing that night and came across that show.

Her story didn't have a happy ending. Her brain tumor was aggressive, and even with the most advanced treatments and medical trials available, this lovely young mother of three died. As I watched her six-month journey, I noticed that she never once said she wished she had cleaned her house more or complained about her cellulite. She embraced her three kids in a way we all should every day. She didn't lament the bad times—she clung to the good ones.

Watching her show seemed to have affected me more deeply than my own experience with a medical scare. I suddenly realized that I had dodged a big bullet.

I found myself thinking about all of the things I would have regretted not doing. I got out my "Life List" and reviewed it with a new sense of passion. I threw the surprise birthday party for my husband I had always wanted to give him; I took that vacation to Italy I had always dreamed of; I took rowing lessons. I looked at my life with new eyes. And I stopped waiting and putting things off.

How often we say that we want to follow our passions and live our dreams someday...but we never know when we will run out of somedays.

"*Before you agree to do anything that might add even the smallest amount of stress to your life, ask yourself: What is my truest intention? Give yourself time to let a 'yes' resound within you. When it's right, I guarantee that your entire body will feel it.*"

~OPRAH WINFREY, media entrepreneur

COMMITMENTS *to* MYSELF

by BJ GALLAGHER

I've always been a "Yes Girl." I'm interested in so many things: I'm eager for fun, creativity, and adventure—and I'm impulsive. So when opportunities come up, I almost always say "yes."

In college, I had trouble choosing a major because so many subjects intrigued me. The catalog of classes looked like a Chinese menu—I wanted to take one from column A, two from column B, and half a dozen from column C. If I'd enrolled in all the classes I wanted to take, I'd be in college decades later!

I have the same problem in a bookstore—so many great books, so little time. What's a girl to do?

And I'm faced with the same dilemma when friends ask me to do things—have lunch, go to the movies, check out this new art exhibit, take in a play, visit the fabulous rose gardens near the university, try a new restaurant, go hear a lecture at the library, attend the opening at a local gallery, and more. Life in Los Angeles is rich with things to do, places to go, people to see— there aren't enough hours in the day!

For many years, the abundance of cultural opportunities left me exhausted and frustrated. I had so many friends, but I didn't have time to spend with all of them. I felt frustrated and guilty.

Finally, out of sheer necessity to save my sanity, I learned a few simple—and effective—ways to solve my problem:

First, I stopped saying "yes" so quickly. Even if I wanted to say "yes" to an invitation, I resisted the urge. Instead, I would say, "I don't have my calendar with me. Let me check and I'll let you know tomorrow, OK?" This way I stalled for time, allowing me to reflect on whether the invitation was something I *really* wanted to do. I didn't let myself feel put on the spot—having to give an instant "yes" or "no." I gave myself some breathing room.

Second, if I didn't want to accept an invitation but didn't want to give a blunt, "No thanks, I don't want to go" answer, I learned to say, "Sorry, I have another commitment." It's a truthful answer, even if my other commitment is to stay home and do nothing. I don't have to explain what my commitment is—it's nobody's business. All I have to say is, "I have a previous commitment."

Which brings me to the third point: Don't explain. Most women—and I'm no exception—have a tendency to explain everything too much. We are socialized to be so sensitive to others' feelings that we go overboard in trying not to hurt anyone—sometimes at the expense of hurting ourselves! We explain why we're late; we explain why we're saying "no" to an invitation; we explain when we have to back out of a commitment; we explain when we're sick and exhausted; *we explain when we don't have to.* We explain excessively because we're afraid that if we don't, someone's feelings will get hurt, or they won't like us. But the truth is, you don't have to explain your reasons for every decision you make—especially decisions about how you choose to spend your time. Try saying, "no thank you, I have another commitment" a few times and resist the urge to explain why.

Just stop talking after you say, "no thanks, can't make it" and see how it works. It'll get easier the more you do it.

Fourth, schedule time on your calendar for "me time." It can be time for a manicure or facial, time for a nap, time to relax and watch your favorite TV show, time to meditate, or time to do nothing at all. Put at least two or three of these appointments on your calendar each week—write them down, don't just think about them, commit them to paper. Then keep them! Keep these appointments as you would an appointment with your doctor or your most important client. Don't cancel your appointments with yourself unless something *really major* comes up.

And finally, remember this: *Other people will treat you only as well as you treat yourself.* Many of us have a bad habit of bailing out on our commitments to ourselves at the drop of a hat. We go to great lengths to keep our commitments to others, but we neglect our commitments to ourselves without a second thought. As therapist and author Dr. Pat Allen says, "The only way you know you love yourself—or anyone else—is by the commitments you are willing to make and keep."

Isn't it time we learn to love ourselves enough to keep our commitments to ourselves?

"*If you don't design your own life plan, chances are you'll fall into someone else's plan. And guess what they have planned for you? Not much.*"

~JIM ROHN, speaker, author

CHAPTER 2

LEARN TO PLAY AGAIN

> *Twenty years from now you will be more disappointed by the things that you didn't do than by the ones you did do. So throw off the bowlines. Sail away from the safe harbor. Catch the trade winds in your sails. Explore. Dream. Discover."*
>
> ~MARK TWAIN, humorist and author

Getting My Spark Back

by ERIKA WESTMORELAND

Life is a wonderful adventure, and you never know where you'll find your inspiration; what actions will lead to what outcomes; and what hidden treasures are waiting just around the corner. I began working with Michelle Sedas in 2003. We weathered our first pregnancies together, with our sons being born four days apart, as well as all of the uncertainties that first-time motherhood brings. Over the next few years, another baby joined the Sedas household and two more precious children joined our family. And so, to manage the stress of juggling the demands of motherhood and working part-time, we began running races together.

In mid-2009, we ran a memorable 10K race. I left my headphones at home and spent the race taking in the sights: observing mothers jogging with their strollers, listening to fellow runners cheering each other on, seeing motivational slogans on the backs of t-shirts. At the time, I felt I wasn't living with much passion. While I was happy with my husband, children and work, still, there was some type of void. And whether it was the electricity in the air, the ambiance of the race, or just being hyped up on endorphins, as I continued to run, I began to reflect on the things that I was truly passionate about.

After the race, Michelle and I had a meaningful conversation about the joys of running and motherhood and giving back to the community. And as the ideas began to fly and the excitement began to build, we knew we had hit on something worthwhile. Realizing that we both shared a strong sense of community, a healthy respect of running, and a deep love of family, we began to form the seeds of *Running Moms Rock*, where our mission is *to inspire moms to live passionately and fearlessly while improving themselves, their families, and their communities in the process.*

Creating *Running Moms Rock* has allowed us to *live inspired.* Michelle says that she wakes up in the middle of the night thinking of ideas for the newsletter or designs for a new t-shirt or which charity we will focus on next. And as for me, I've always been a person who has a lot of ideas. But, this was the first time that everything just seemed to come together. I'm so excited about this company and how it is inspiring us as moms to be our best selves while allowing us to collectively give back to the community. Before we started this company, I was living, but I wasn't truly living passionately. Forming this company has allowed my spark to come back. Like I say, life is a wonderful adventure, and you just never know what treasures are waiting just around the corner. ♪

"I define joy as a sense of well-being and internal peace— a connection to what matters.**"**

~OPRAH WINFREY, media entreprenuer

Go Jump In the Lake

by LISA HAMMOND

Learning to unplug hasn't come easily for me. The mere thought of being sans cell phone and laptop originally made my pulse race and gave me a rash. However, over time I have come to look forward to the one time each year when I truly leave the rat race and go jump in the lake!

Every summer for almost a decade we have gone to glorious Lake Powell. There are no phones, no cellular connections, and e-mail won't work either. While out on the lake, we are in our own little world. Turns out there are some places even stress can't find you.

Lake Powell is near the Grand Canyon and just as stunning. Camping there gives me the chance to spend time reconnecting with nature. Spending nights under a ceiling of stars surrounded by walls of sheer red cliffs and a fluid carpet of deep green water is nirvana.

The first year we made this trip was quite an adventure. Not only because we were out of contact for the first time, but we had never piloted a houseboat either! Piloting a houseboat is kinda like driving a bus—on water! I only wish we had video-taped the many mishaps and fiascoes we had. I am certain we could have won a funniest home video contest!

Cooking also became an adventure. We found you could BBQ just about anything! We discovered you could cook everything from pancakes to lasagna over a BBQ. The kids, of course, thought we had lost our minds!

Over the years our trips to Lake Powell have morphed and changed as the kids grew up and went to college. We have gone from youngsters playing in the sand, to teenagers and wild wakeboarding, to our now more mellow trips involving more floating and reading than boat riding.

But do you want to know what the best part of every trip is? No makeup, no hair dryer, swimsuit required—clothing optional. Heck, if I brush my teeth in the morning I really think I have gone all out! I am always amazed at how liberating it is not to have to think about what I look like, to simply shower, brush my hair and be done—you know, like men get to do every day! Imagine having your complete bag of tricks consist of a comb every day!

I would never have guessed that the best part of the trip would be not having to "get ready" each day. How did we get that phrase in our vocabulary? What are we getting ready for?

When was the last time you did something really spontaneous? Where has your spirit of adventure gone? If the answer is "buried somewhere deep," it is time to let her out!

I have discovered the more I carve out time for reflection, dreaming and play, the more effective I am in all areas of my life.

"*If we could see the miracle of a single flower clearly, our whole life would change.*" ~THE BUDDHA

CHAPTER 3

ASK FOR HELP

> *It is true that no one can harm that person who wears armor. But no one can help him either."*
>
> ~KRISTIN HUNTER, novelist

Hanging Up
the Superwoman Cape

by BJ GALLAGHER

"**Y**our problem, Mom, is that you never let people contribute to you," my son Michael said to me a few years ago. "You're all about helping other people but you never let anyone help you. You say, 'Oh, no thanks, I can handle it.' It's very frustrating for people who try to contribute to your life."

I came face-to-face with the wisdom of his words last year when I needed a total hip replacement. The pain in my hip got progressively worse for about five years until it reached the point where I could barely walk. I hobbled around, grimacing in pain, popping pain medication like it was candy. Surgery became my only alternative.

I scheduled the date ... then postponed it twice. "I have a busy life," I explained to the scheduling nurse. "It's just not convenient for me to have surgery." She and I both knew that there would *never* be a convenient time for someone like me. When I finally scheduled the third date, I decided that I was going to have to keep it, whether I wanted to or not.

I began to make preparations—donating my own blood for surgery; rearranging furniture in my house so that I could get around on a walker; stocking up on cases of cat food and bags of kitty litter; buying four-inch cushions to raise the seating level of all the chairs; and buying an ever-so-attractive raised toilet seat for the bathroom. That was the easy part.

Then came the hard part—asking for the help I knew I would need while I was in the hospital and when I came home. I told all my neighbors and friends that I didn't want to be alone during the first week of recovery at home. I was afraid I might fall down and not be able to call for help. So I put out the word and asked that people come by and baby-sit me.

Next, I asked seven different neighbors to walk my dog one day a week for a month—that way, the responsibility of dog-walking wouldn't fall all on one person. I even included a couple friends whose dogs had died within the past year, thinking that they'd probably like a little doggie love without having to get a new dog of their own.

I set aside money to have my cleaning lady come every week for three months, instead of the usual twice a month. I asked my son to plant some lovely plants in the garden so that it would be pretty and nice to sit outside while I was recuperating. I asked various friends to come see me in the hospital, and scheduled them so that they came at different times on different days.

I was unaccustomed to asking people for help, but discovered it really wasn't so hard. And when the day of my surgery came, I went into the hospital feeling calm and relaxed, knowing that I had asked for the help I needed and everyone would do their part.

Some people even went above and beyond the call of what I had asked them—my friends Julie and Marty Bagish each donated blood on my behalf, in addition to keeping me company on my first day after surgery. I was so touched by their generosity—it isn't everyone who will literally give you their blood!

After I came home, the whole first week of recovery was just wonderful. There were people in my house all day and into the evening—it was like a non-stop party. My refrigerator has never been so full of wonderful food, as friends and neighbors trooped into my kitchen with homemade quiche, take-out Italian food, bags of groceries, mango sorbet and tasty treats of all kinds. Even my 84-year-old dad drove two hours to see me and washed my hair in the kitchen sink when I asked him to.

My son Michael stayed with me every night and helped me in and out of bed when I had to use the bathroom. I felt terrible because he had to get up and go to work every morning, after being up and down with me several times during the night. But my wise friend Anita Goldstein admonished me, "Don't feel guilty. It's payback…and it's good training." We both laughed.

After a couple weeks of recovery, I was able to give up the walker and use a cane to get around. I recall saying to Michael, "I have never felt so loved in all my life."

He looked at me and replied, "That says something about you, Mom. All these people are a reflection of the love you've given them. But this is the first time you've ever let them contribute to you."

My son, the wise old soul. He didn't get that from me.

"Three of the most powerful words in the English language are: 'Please help me.'"

~CATHY CONHEIM, therapist, author

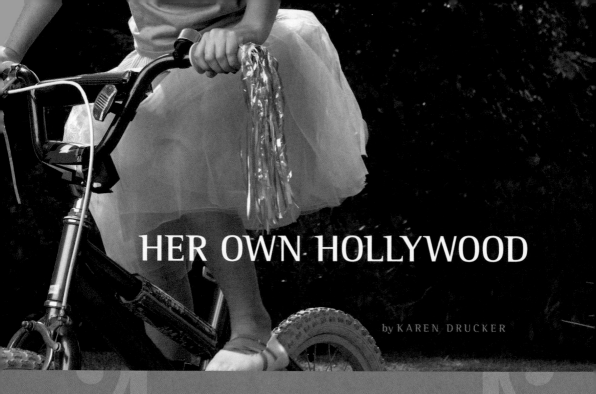

HER OWN HOLLYWOOD

by KAREN DRUCKER

I never realized what a unique and different childhood I had until I moved away to college. Growing up in Laurel Canyon in the '60s was a mix of a hippie haven, with little bungalows in the trees, and some nice houses, but overall a pretty relaxed and funky area. Many famous people lived in Laurel Canyon at the time including Joni Mitchell, Elliott Gould, director Hal Ashby and Carole King. I spent long afternoons walking my dogs, and sitting on a hill for hours gazing out at the legendary

Hollywood Sign, imagining all the stories that went along with old Hollywood.

The Hollywood sign was falling into disrepair and when I heard that they were planning to tear it down due to lack of funds, I was shocked. How could this be? This sign was a symbol of Hollywood and the movies. People travel from all over the world to see this landmark sign. The 13-year-old entrepreneur in me knew that I had to do something. I still don't know what possessed me to do this, but I decided to organize a bike ride to raise funds to save the sign. Now that I look back on this idea, I have so much admiration for the naiveté of kids. Raising the hundreds of thousands of dollars this project would cost was not even in my realm of thinking. I just knew that they wanted to tear down my sign, and it was up to ME to save it!

I gathered all my friends together and explained the whole plan for the bike ride. Everyone took on jobs including publicity, mapping out the bike course, making up the pledge forms, and getting our junior high school on board. I had the idea that if we could have some big name stars show up, it would generate more interest. I wrote letters to a bunch of stars, with no luck. I went to the Friday afternoon taping of the Carol Burnett show and sent a letter backstage to her. I got a nice rejection letter back. Somehow, however, through some of these contacts, I got my star for the day—"Ms. Hollywood." I had no idea who she was, but it looked good on the flyer. A few local TV stations even promised they would show up and cover the event.

The day came for the bike ride, and about a hundred kids showed up with bikes and pledge forms ranging from $20 to $100. About 15 minutes before the ride was supposed to start, a vision in skin-tight, hot-pink hot pants, purple-spandex tube top, and chunky platform heels, walked toward me. Just about all the kids fell off their bikes watching her. Our school was located right below Hollywood Boulevard with its interesting characters, to say the least, and my first thought was that one of the locals was going to create a scene at our event.

She came up to me, extended her long pink, fake-finger-nailed hand to me and, with a voice just like Marilyn Monroe, said, "Hi there. I am Ms. Hollywood, and I am here to help you save the sign!" The kid in me was a bit shocked, but the producer in me knew that the media would love this and she would guarantee that we would make the evening news.

At the appointed time, the bikers got into place, Ms. Hollywood lifted the flag, and in a surprisingly drill sergeant-type manner let rip a, "Ready, Set, Go!" The kids were off, the media got their footage, and I started adding up the pledge forms.

Everyone had a good time, and on Monday morning I triumphantly walked into the Hollywood Chamber of Commerce to drop off a big pile of cash, reveling in the fact that we had saved the sign! When the clerk counted out the $700 we raised, she gave me a look of pity mixed with motherly pride. She gently explained that it would take a whole lot more to save the sign, and that I should feel good for at least trying.

I walked out of there feeling dejected and depressed. I felt like I had failed all the kids that had joined me in this project. After a lot of, "Well, we tried," we all moved on and waited for the announcement of when the sign would be torn down.

As with most things political and civic, the actual planning of the demolition of the sign took months, with all the red tape and bidding wars of who would do it. The delays gave local businesses time to join forces and eventually, because of all the publicity and heated debates about the importance of this icon, enough money was raised and the sign was saved after all. The Hollywood Chamber of Commerce gave me a little plaque for my efforts, and I found out that the two main businesses that contributed the most money heard about it through our bike ride.

I realize now, so many years later, what a gift that whole experience was to me. I love the quote from Mother Teresa, "We cannot do great things, only small things with great love." Even though I am sure that my parents and teachers knew that whatever money we could raise would just be a drop in the bucket for the amount needed to save the sign, they encouraged all of us to do whatever we could. I think that I am still doing that to this day. I want to be a person who makes a difference, who helps others fill their lamps, lift their spirits, and encourages other women. I try to do what I can to change this world.

And the Hollywood sign? It's still there, presiding over an ever-changing city, regal and shining. Whenever I go home, I look at it and just smile.

WE ARE THE ONES
Words & Music From Karen Drucker's CD "Shine"

We are the ones we've been waiting for.
We are the ones who will make a difference.
We are the ones who will change the world.
We are the ones, we are, we are.
We are the ones, we are, we are.

I've been feelin' like I can't make a difference.
Been feelin' like there ain't no use.
Feelin' tired and a little unconscious,
coming up with every kind of excuse.
'Till I realized it's not all up to me,
when we join together we shape our destiny,
to see a world where we are living as one.
It can be, it shall be, it will be done.

CHAPTER 4

MASTER THE ART
OF DOING
NOTHING

"*Don't underestimate the value of doing nothing, of just going along, listening to all the things you can't hear, and not bothering.*"
~WINNIE THE POOH

4

Detox

by BARBARA JENSEN

The phone rang, rousing me from my drowsy sunbathing. I reached for the cordless phone next to the glass of iced tea on the table beside my chaise lounge.

"Hello," I said when I answered the phone.

"What are you doing?" I heard my mother ask.

"I'm detoxing," I said sleepily.

"From what?" she asked.

"From my life. It's only been four days since I left my big corporate job. I need time to get all the poison out of my system. It was such a frustrating place to work. The five years I spent there took a huge toll and the way they handled my buy-out was so painful …I need time to get rid of all the negative feelings. So I'm lying here in the backyard, letting the sun bake those feelings out of me."

"How long will it take?" Mom asked.

"I don't know. It takes what it takes, I guess. It took me a long time to get so angry…I guess it'll take some time to process and get rid of my anger and resentment."

"OK then," she said, not knowing quite how to respond.

"Don't worry, Mom," I reassured her. "I just need to do nothing for awhile. Sunbathe, hang out with friends, watch soaps on TV, take naps, read, take long walks, meditate, go to the movies or art museums—it's all good."

"I hope you're using sunscreen," Mom said.

"Yes, Mom."

My mother didn't really understand my need to do nothing. She was worried about my future and thought I should be out looking for a new job. But I knew that if I didn't take time to detox, I'd carry all that negative energy with me on job interviews and that would be a very bad thing. People are sensitive to others' energy and no one was going to hire me if I came in the door loaded down with old baggage.

Sometimes, the best thing is to catch a few rays, take a little snooze, and let time heal your wounds. Oh, and don't forget your sunscreen.

"*Doing nothing is better than being busy doing nothing.*"

~LAO TZU, Chinese Taoist philosopher

"Sitting quietly, doing nothing, spring comes, and the grass grows by itself."

~ZEN PROVERB

How to Light Up a Room

by BJ GALLAGHER

"**S**mart bosses hire people as much for their potential as their experience," a former boss of mine used to say. "If you want people to be stimulated, challenged, and eager to grow on the job, you want to look at their potential more than their specific experience. If you hire only those who have done the exact same job before, they'll be bored within a year or two and they won't be contributing much."

He practiced what he preached. He hired me to be the manager of training and development for a large university in Los Angeles. I found out a year or so later what he had told his boss: "She doesn't know anything about training but she sure knows how to light up a room."

Now, in his defense (and mine), I wasn't totally without qualifications. I had been on campus for ten years—first as a student, then grad student, and finally, on staff as a continuing education specialist. I knew everyone on campus and how to cut through the bureaucratic red tape to get things done. I was superb at managing budgets, writing promotional materials to advertise classes and managing student workers. I was well-respected and well-liked by faculty and staff alike.

What I didn't know was the difference between education and training, but I was a quick study and my new boss understood that. He could teach me the parts of the job that I didn't know. And I could teach him the ins and outs of the campus, since he was new there. We were a good team.

But as with any job, all was not perfect. Like any department at a college or university, our budget was always too small for what we wanted to accomplish. I had student workers instead of full-time staff, which meant that I was frequently getting a new crop of kids to train—which took time and energy. I had to find creative ways to get faculty to teach workshops and seminars for employees, since I had no money to pay them for extra work. There were days when I felt like it was all just too much. I felt like Sisyphus eternally pushing a boulder uphill. Some days I just ran out of steam.

It was on such days that I would recall what my boss had said about me. At the end of the day, I'd head across campus to the faculty center where they had a small pub for faculty and senior staff. "I'm going to go see if I can still light up a room," I'd mutter to myself. Feeling totally depleted, I'd drag myself into the pub, walk to the bar to order a glass of wine, and scan the room for a place to sit. Usually, someone would catch my eye and motion me to come sit with them.

After an hour or two, I'd leave the faculty center feeling happy—though still tired. It never failed. I knew I had lit up the room and felt reassured that I hadn't lost my touch.

Of course, what was really happening is that people in the room were lighting ME up. I was feeding off their friendship, their smiles, their attention, and their energy. After all, a light bulb doesn't light itself up—it has to be plugged into a socket so that electricity can flow to it. And that's what was happening to me—I plugged myself into the energy of my friends and colleagues.

I learned that lighting up a room isn't about doing anything—it's really more about just being—being connected to other people. I can just sit and do nothing as I let them replenish the oil in my lamp, the charge in my battery, the water in my well. I came to understand that I can light up rooms because I get charged up with the energy of friendship and love.

CHAPTER 5

RECHARGE AND REJOICE!

"If you neglect to recharge a battery, it dies. And if you run full speed ahead without stopping for water, you lose momentum to finish the race."

~OPRAH WINFREY, media entrepreneur

Creative Play

by BJ GALLAGHER

Creativity is a mystery to me. I don't understand exactly what it is or how it works. It seems to be some sort of energy, like electricity, that I can't see but I can feel its energy and see its effects. Being in the flow of creativity is a mystical experience … feeling in sync with life forces and the universe. It's relaxing, refreshing, restorative. One of the most exhilarating experiences I've had with the renewing power of creativity occurred when I took a class on furniture painting.

I like functional art—colorful, pretty things that I can wear, drink from, sit on, eat out of, or use in some practical way. I love ordinary objects transformed through artistic creativity. I also think that somewhere inside me is an artist who is trying to get out. I can't draw or paint on canvas very well, but perhaps I could find some other art form that I could try. I thought maybe furniture painting could be my medium, so I signed up for a class through the Learning Annex and went off one Saturday to my painting adventure.

We were instructed to bring a small piece of old furniture for our class project. I brought a yard sale coffee table. Our instructor gave us the basics and we began painting—first the base colors, then the decorative designs on top.

As I worked, I remembered another class I'd taken, called "The Artist's Way." And what I remembered was, "You have to give yourself permission to make bad art before you can make good art."

"Bad art?" I said to myself, "I can do that." So I gave myself permission to use my coffee table as a trial and error piece, a sampler, an experiment, an opportunity to explore this new art form.

We painted all day, taking a break for lunch. At the end of the class, my table was not done. So, I bought some more paint from the shop where the class was held, and took my table home to finish.

I had a bite of dinner and resumed painting. I was on a roll. I was having so much fun—painting flowers, squiggles, words, phrases, dots, symbols, textures, and colors all over the table—even the underside. I decided not to go to bed until it was done. I wanted to stay in the flow.

The hours rolled by and I kept painting; lost in my fun and lost in time. Finally, it was finished. I was happy. I went to the kitchen and glanced at a clock—it was 3 a.m.! I was shocked. Never in my life have I gotten so immersed in anything that I lost track of time. What an amazing experience! It was as if time fell away while I was in the flow of painting. You've heard of out-of-body experiences? Well, this was an out-of-time experience.

I came away from it with a new appreciation for the joy of the creative process and what it's like to be in the flow. I loved it. I felt completely happy, at peace, free from any worldly cares and concerns. Any stress I had, had now disappeared.

And I had a new coffee table.

"*Recharging can be done with the ones you love. Turn off the TV, turn off the radio, turn down the lights, pop some popcorn, put on comfortable clothes, get out the Table Topics questions and take turns sharing answers about life, aspirations, memories, hopes and dreams. This is one of my favorite things to do with my 30-year-old son, and he loves it! We learn a lot about each other, and we remember those evenings vs. losing precious time zoning in front of the TV.*" ~DAWN EVERLY

COME HELL *or* HIGH WATER

by LISA HAMMOND

It all began because of a rant at dinner. For months I had been trying to have lunch with a girlfriend. It seemed like a simple enough concept, meet up at a local café for a quick salad to catch up. Five months later we still had yet to find a date on either calendar when we were both free on the same day. Then my poor husband made the mistake at dinner one night of announcing that he had managed to pull together a group of eight men to go to Scotland on a golf trip—in less than a week!

How was that possible? I ranted and raved all through dinner! How in the world had he managed to get eight men to coordinate their schedules in less than a week? I couldn't manage to set a lunch date with one woman and I had been trying for over 20 weeks! Why is it that men can so easily drop everything without a second thought and fly halfway around the world to hang out with their friends and we can't get away for lunch without an act of Congress?

That was it! Come hell or high water I was going to plan my own girls' trip! Women need—we deserve—to charge our batteries too. I called my friend Paula and asked her to go to dinner with me to plan our first trip. Over wine we became the el capitans of our girls' trip! As fate would have it, a woman overheard us talking and said she couldn't resist telling us about her group who gets together every year. She said they call themselves the "Houseboat Hussies," because they meet up on a friend's houseboat each year. Well, that was all the inspiration we needed to become the "Hell or High Water Hussies," because come hell or high water we were going to put together a girls' trip!

It took some coaxing and educating to get women to understand just how vital it is to make time for themselves, but we now we have a loyal group who makes the trip each year. We have taken trips from Canada to Catalina. We've had some incredible experiences and the friendships that have formed are ones I will always cherish. But most importantly, I have learned the invaluable lesson that comes from making recharging my battery a priority.

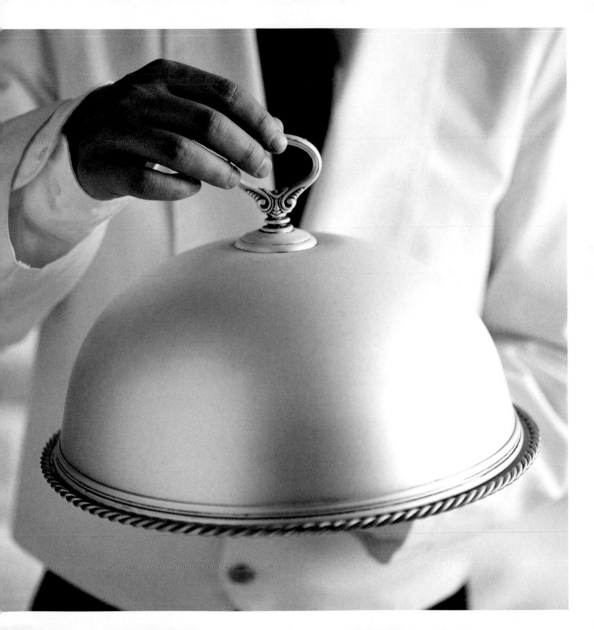

"Your time is limited, so don't waste it living someone else's life. Don't be trapped by dogma—which is living with the results of other people's thinking. Don't let the noise of others' opinions drown out your own inner voice. And most important, have the courage to follow your heart and intuition. They somehow already know what you truly want to become. Everything else is secondary."

~STEVE JOBS, founder and CEO of Apple

Australian author Anthea Paul wrote: "Commitment is emotional intent backed up by action. Commitment isn't something you pledge; it's something you do."

It is our deepest wish that you find commitment in your own life—more precisely, that you make a commitment TO your life.

It's wonderful that you love your family—your spouse and/or kids—your friends and other loved ones. But it's important that you love yourself MORE. It's critical that you love yourself FIRST. After all, we already know what happens when we love others more than ourselves—when we put everyone else's needs first and our own needs last. And we know that if nothing changes, nothing changes.

We have written this book as a call to action for you and the women you influence. People respect you when they see you draw healthy boundaries. The men in your life are more likely to cherish you when they see that you cherish yourself. Teach your daughters, nieces and granddaughters that they are the stars in their own lives. We hope that you will be an inspiring role model for your girlfriends by BEING the change you wish to see in all women.

As we end this book, we want to leave you with a final gift—your very own "The Real Woman Creed." Take it to heart; post it where you'll see it frequently; share it with others. Declare yourself the center of your own universe—committed to keeping your flame burning brightly as you light up the world.

THE REAL WOMAN CREED©

I believe that within me lies an extraordinary radiance, and I commit to letting my light loose in the world.

I believe that the source of my power and wisdom is in the center of my being, and I commit to acting from this place of strength.

I believe that I possess an abundance of passion and creative potential, and I commit to the expression of these gifts.

I believe that the time has come to let go of old notions and unhealthy attitudes, and I commit to re-examine what I have been told about beauty and dismiss what insults my soul.

I believe that negative thoughts and words compromise my well-being, and I commit to thinking and speaking positively about myself and others.

I believe that young women are in need of positive role models, and I commit to being an example of authenticity and self-love.

I believe in the relationship between my well-being and the well-being of the planet, and I commit to a life of mindfulness that regards all living things as holy and worthy of my love.

I believe it is my spiritual responsibility to care for my body with respect, kindness and compassion, and I commit to balancing my life in such a way that my physical being is fully expressed and nurtured.

I believe that joy is an essential part of wellness, and I commit to removing obstacles to joy and creating a life that is full of exuberance.

I believe that a woman who loves herself is a powerful, passionate, attractive force, and I commit, from this day forward, to loving myself deeply and extravagantly.

Written by Jan Phillips | © Real Woman Project | www.realwomenproject.org

ABOUT *the* AUTHORS

LISA HAMMOND, Lisa Hammond, known as The Barefoot CEO, has a passion to inspire and uplift women and girls and a mission to give back. Since selling her company Femail Creations in 2010 Lisa's focus has been writing inspirational books. She is living out her Life List and challenging others to do the same.

Among the many awards Lisa is most proud to have received include The National Association of Moms In Business Create Your Dreams Award, the Soroptimist International Business & Organizations "Advancing the Status of Women Award" and the SBA "Business Person of the Year Award."

Lisa's books *Oil for Your Lamp* and *Oh Thank Goodness It's Not Just Me* (Simple Truths) both speak to the common experiences all women share and can relate to. Lisa's book *Dream Big: Finding the Courage to Follow Your Dreams and Laugh at Your Nightmares* (Conari Press) remains a best-seller and is now available on Kindle and Ipad. *Lisa's Permission to Dream Journal* (Conari Press) is used in workshops across the country. Lisa turned her passion for inspirational quotes into her *Stepping Stones collection* (Red Wheel Weiser), now both available as an APP for your phone.

Hammond, her books and companies have often been featured on television, various syndicated radio programs, and in many national magazines including: *O the Oprah Magazine, In Touch magazine, Women's Day,* and on the cover of *Business Week.*

Lisa is a dynamic keynote speaker and workshop presenter all around the country for clients such as Eli Lilly, the National Association of Women Business Owners, and American Express.

FOR MORE INFORMATION, VISIT LISA'S POPULAR BLOG, WITH OVER 300,000 ONLINE SUBSCRIBERS:

www.thebarefootceo.com OR **www.oilforyourlamp.com**

You can follow Lisa on Twitter @thebarefootceo and @oilforyourlamp

BJ GALLAGHER is an inspirational author and speaker. She writes business books that educate and empower, women's books that enlighten and entertain, gift books that inspire and inform, and kids' books that charm and delight. Whether her audience is corporate executives, working women, or a group of giggling youngsters, her message is powerful, positive and practical. She motivates and teaches with empathy, understanding, and more than a little humor.

BJ's international best-seller, *A Peacock in the Land of Penguins* (Berrett-Koehler; third edition 2001), has sold over 320,000 copies in 23 languages. Her most recent books include:

~ *It's Never Too Late to Be What You Might Have Been* (Viva Editions; 2009)

~ *Why Don't I Do the Things I Know Are Good For Me?* (Berkley; 2009)

~ *Learning to Dance in the Rain* (Simple Truths; 2009)

~ *The Best Way Out is Always Through* (Simple Truths; 2009)

BJ and her books have been featured on CBS Evening News with Bob Schieffer, the Today Show with Matt Lauer, Fox News, PBS, CNN, and other television and radio programs. She is quoted almost weekly in various newspapers, women's magazines, and websites, including: *O the Oprah Magazine, Redbook, Woman's World, Ladies Home Journal, First for Women, New York Times, Chicago Tribune, Wall Street Journal, Christian Science Monitor, Orlando Sentinel, Financial Times* (U.K.), *The Guardian* (U.K.), CareerBuilder.com, MSNBC.com and CNN.com.

In addition to writing books, BJ also conducts seminars and delivers keynotes at conferences across the country. Her clients include: IBM, Chevron, U.S. Veterans Administration, John Deere Credit Canada, Volkswagen, Farm Credit Services of America, Raytheon, U.S. Department of Interior, Phoenix Newspapers Inc., the American Press Institute, Infiniti, Nissan, U.S. Army, Atlanta Journal Constitution, among others.

FOR MORE INFORMATION, VISIT BJ'S WEB SITES:

**www.womenneed2know.com   www.bjgallagher.com
www.peacockproductions.com**

The Simple Truths Difference

If you have enjoyed this book we invite you
to check out our entire collection of gift books, with free
inspirational movies, at www.simpletruths.com.
You'll discover it's a great way to inspire friends and family,
or to thank your best customers and employees.